MIDDLESEX RHYMES

Edited By Megan Roberts

First published in Great Britain in 2018 by:

 Young**Writers**

Young Writers
Remus House
Coltsfoot Drive
Peterborough
PE2 9BF
Telephone: 01733 890066
Website: www.youngwriters.co.uk

FOREWORD

Young Writers was created in 1991 with the express purpose of promoting and encouraging creative writing. Each competition we create is tailored to the relevant age group, hopefully giving each child the inspiration and incentive to create their own piece of writing, whether it's a poem or a short story. We truly believe that seeing it in print gives pupils a sense of achievement and pride in their work and themselves.

Our latest competition, Monster Poetry, focuses on uncovering the different techniques used in poetry and encouraging pupils to explore new ways to write a poem. Using a mix of imagination, expression and poetic styles, this anthology is an impressive snapshot of the inventive, original and skilful writing of young people today. These poems showcase the creativity and talent of these budding new writers as they learn the skills of writing, and we hope you are as entertained by them as we are.

CONTENTS

22 Pawandeep Singh Takawal (11)   66
23 Harsweet Randhawa (10)   67
24 Esha K Khosa (10)   68
24 Ravneet Kaur Khaira (9)   69
25 Jasraj Singh Bajaj (7)   70
26 Sharanpreet Kaur Sahota (9)   71
27 Sehajveer Sethi (11)   72
28 Nimret Kaur Jandu (11)   73
29 Simleen Kaur Sachdev (11)   74
30 Harvir Singh (9)   75
31 Jagdeep Singh (9)   76
32 Gunveen Kaur Arora (11)   77
33 Gurpreet Singh Rajwansi (10)   78
34 Attar Kaur Hanspal (11)   79
35 Navneet Kaur (11)   80
36 Karanbeer Bhullar (8)   81
37 Arshpreet Sehdev (9)   82
38 Kirtan Kaur Dhaliwal (10)   83
39 Harjan Singh (11)   84
40 Manchit Singh Grover (11)   85
41 Jaiveer Chana (9)   86
42 Simar Kaur (10)   87
43 Simrit Somal (10)   88
44 Navkiran Kaur Virdee (10)   89
45 Jasmeet Kaur Sekhon (9)   90
46 Harkamal Singh (9)   91
47 Falguni Sodhi (10)   92
48 Harsimran Kaur (10)   93
49 Gurleen Singh (10)   94
50 Mannat Kaur Kohli (9)   95
51 Sukhman Kaur Sandhu (10)   96
52 Chavleen Chopra (8) BFF   97
53 Khushpreet Hoonjan (10)   98
54 Simran Kaur Phull (11)   99
55 Sanam Sachdev (9)   100
56 Rythamdeep Thind (7)   101
57 Dipneet Kaur (11)   102
58 Avneet Kaur Chawla (7)   103
59 Ramneek Kaur Grewal (10)   104
60 Jagdeep Singh Virdee (10)   105
61 Angelina Kapur (8)   106
62 Jasveen Kaur Singh (9)   107
63 Amraj Singh Dhaliwal (10)   108

64 Nitika Sharma (8)   109
65 Mannat Sedana (8)   110
66 Seerat Monjal (9)   111
67 Tegh Kaur Rao (9)   112

St Michael's CE Primary School, Brigadier Hill

Harrison Sykes (8)   113

St Richard Reynolds Catholic College, Twickenham

Emeline Gec (8)   114
Lakeisha-Jayne Seenauth (8)   115
Anne-Marie Kostov (8)   116
Milo Ketteringham (7)   117
Maisie Marsden (9)   118
Elsie Kinch (8)   120
Olivia Swiderska (8)   122
Finbar Harris (8)   123
Bianka Krystina Szabat (9)   124
Bosley Brown (8)   126
Saskia Fahey (9)   127
Lewis Fitzgerald-Monk (9)   128
Nikola Nycz (8)   129
Charlotte Rose Ball (8)   130
Harry Ibbs (8)   131
Sienna Minhas (7)   132
Liza Coimbra (8)   133
Charlie McKenzie (9)   134
Rosetta Piercy (9)   135
Huxley Kinch (9)   136
Theo Corth (8)   137
Nerea Whitmore (9)   138
Daniel James Atkinson (8)   139
Freya Hughes (9)   140
Miguel Ángel Mendoza Estrada (7)   141
Casper Hillier (8)   142
Liana Minhas (7)   143
Finlay Kinch (9)   144
Scarlett Nicol (9)   145
James Hazard (8)   146

Euan Fitgerald-Monk (7)	147
Liam Jack Jeffers (9)	148
Benjamin Norman (8)	149
Maria Shakaj (8)	150
Ethan Nicol (7)	151
Jack Bunney (8)	152
Isabel Bunney (8)	153
Ella Payne-Traverso (8)	154
Albert Connors (7)	155
Luca Gasparini (8)	156
Len Mundow (9)	157
Susanna Benedetto (7)	158

Viking Primary School, Northolt

Mohamed Hussein (9)	159
Jaasiel Opeoluwa Olosinmo (9)	160
Raheem Kaoud (9)	161
Yakub Mustapha (9)	162
Emuovweoghene Clement Ewruie (9)	163
Wiktoria Orzycka (9)	164
Mustafa Osmani (8)	165
Yonis Arab (8)	166

THE POEMS

Ugly

I once was born,
Hiding by a lawn,
I'm quite a craze,
I'm the size of a maze.
Other monsters think I'm funny, furry,
And of course, always in a hurry,
Holding people's bag,
With a lovely, tough tag.
Girls do their hair,
It's my worst nightmare,
Thinking and winking, what to do?
Then they start to sing, 'skip to my lou'!

Huda Elmi (9)
Allenby Primary School, Southall

The Scary Yet Good Monster

All night and day he roars and growls,
He can make you scared and make you howl,
He lurks in the cave, within your sight,
Frozen, you stare and wait for a fright.
He quickly runs towards you,
With his big, beady eyes,
You run away and start to cry,
In your dream, he's definitely awake,
With his thick purple skin, stinky long tongue,
His hairy horns, and giant eyes.
You think you know who and what it is.
You think for a moment then know who it is,
You look back in your dream to see where he is,
You look and glare around.
"Oh no, I know where he is."
You fall back asleep, he's eating a mouse,
"Argh! He's in my house!"
He breathes out fire, flames of red,
"Can I play with you?" the monster said.

Lara Wissam Cherri (10)

Chase Bridge Primary School, Twickenham

The Dancing Dragon

Was it a bird? Was it a plane?
Or was it a magic flying train?
It flew and it flapped its mighty wings,
And his scaly arms had big blue rings.
It landed on a hill,
It filled me with a thrill,
As I looked to see a big, dancing dragon.
He swayed his tail to the song,
I ran to him and danced along,
The music really caught my ear,
Maybe, one day, we could come back here.
Then, I saw him fly into the sky,
I yelled to him, "Bye!"
And I gave a sigh.
I went back home,
I felt quite alone,
I really missed the dancing dragon.

Beata Gorecka (10)
Chase Bridge Primary School, Twickenham

Friend Or Foe?

I was walking down the street one day,
Something stared at me,
I looked into its googly eyes,
I wondered what it could be.
I thought I saw a strip of pink,
But then, I smelt an unusual stink,
Should I go and say hello,
To that little blob of yellow?
I tiptoed over, very slow,
And then I saw a special glow,
What could this mystery creature be?
I'm really glad that I went to see.
A beautiful monster like a rainbow,
With long, silky hair, and a JoJo bow!
Now there's one thing I know,
She is a friend and not a foe.

Brooke Bridger (10)
Chase Bridge Primary School, Twickenham

Demons Can Be Anything!

There was a demon with talons,
Fangs and three eyes,
It was stinky, scary, short and fluffy.
He came from the depths of a dark,
Black hole and was naughty and short,
And never had a bath.
He could swim and fly,
And had a really long tongue,
And when he ate food,
He did a big, loud burp.
He had a very big mouth,
And never stopped talking,
He was mean and spotty,
And, when he talked to people,
They ran away screaming.
They'd pray, and pray, and pray for help,
But he chased them on his hairy, short legs.

Jack Weedon (10)
Chase Bridge Primary School, Twickenham

Googly Gong Day

Googly Gong is from Planet Gorf,
Googly Gong has colourful horns,
Although Googly Gong has lots of legs,
He really doesn't eat many eggs.
One day, Googly dug and dug,
Until he spotted a little green bug,
He was supposed to find his favourite stone,
But in the end, he just walked home.
Googly Gong's house was dark and dull,
But I saw something fall onto his skull.
Googly Gong is very stinky,
So I think he's not that pretty,
Googly Gong is very tired,
But I don't feel very inspired.

Amisha Sharma (9)
Chase Bridge Primary School, Twickenham

Are You Bad?

Imagine is bad,
Maybe a bit mad,
But don't be sad,
Because I'll tell you something,
That will make you glad.
Imagine had something to tell me,
He had a secret you see,
He came up to me with a gift.
Imagine gave me a cake,
And I knew I wasn't going to shake,
If anyone goes to him I shall,
Tell them he is good after all.

Ruby Anne Pyke (10)
Chase Bridge Primary School, Twickenham

Fumble The Friend

This monster is from a mysterious, eerie and scary
planet,
He used to have no friends,
Because he was selfish, horrible and cruel to
others,
Even his mother.
One day, on Fumble's birthday,
No one came to his party,
He was all alone,
Going mad and feeling sad.
So he decided to be kind,
And the monsters didn't mind,
Giving him a second chance,
So they all danced.
Fumble had an amazing, brilliant,
And fun birthday party,
Now Fumble is nice, friendly and gentle,
Therefore he has lots of friends,
And everyone likes him,
Even Grim, the nasty one,
Who hates every monster.

Before Fumble was mean,
But now he is keen to please everyone,
Fumble lives in a cave and he is very brave,
If you ever see him,
Give him a hug as he is not a thug.

Arya Jhawer (9)
Cranford Primary School, Cranford

Friendly Monster

It was a sizzling, scintillating day,
I was out to play,
Beautiful spring was around,
Daffodils nodding in the ground.
Suddenly, there were rustling sounds,
Through the shrubs with bounds,
Out sprang a mammoth, mechanical monster,
As huge as an ocean whale, eating a lobster.
It gave me nothing but a shake,
And I dropped my yummy cake.
He said, "I am not like others, I am calm,
Never before have I caused harm,
Sunny is my name, I am simple and plain,
See? No tresses, I don't wear dresses.
I knew that would make you smile,
You see, that's my style.
Let's have some fun, one on one,
Take a chance, let's dance!
Or slide on me, and we'll glide, just you and me."

Surya Teja Pachipulusu (9)
Cranford Primary School, Cranford

Poor Frite

There was once a monster called Frite,
He played a lot and didn't like to fight,
Everyone very much hated him.
He didn't like exercise or going to the gym,
Although he was hated by everyone, he was nice,
He often was quiet like a group of mice.
Everyone thought Frite was under their bed,
He was often a little underfed.
He liked making things and he was fast like The Flash,
He was really poor and didn't have cash,
Frite was really filled with mites.
One of his hobbies was flying kites,
He could fly and breathe fire,
He was also part tiger.
Everyone thought Frite was under their bed,
Frite was a little fed,
Although he was hated, he was nice,
He was really good and nice.

Yunus Sheikh (9)
Cranford Primary School, Cranford

The Bubblegum Mermaid

The Bubblegum Mermaid was born,
In a deep blue and dark sea.
It has peach skin,
And blue eyes that glow,
It smells like bubblegum,
And has straight teeth,
It is kind and pretty.
She left the sea for an adventure,
It wanted to be attractive,
And make people happy.
But it met me first,
It played with me until it had to go home,
It sizzled into the sand,
And shouted, "Bye everyone!"
Everyone was happy after she left,
And exclaimed,
"Bye beautiful bubblegum mermaid!"
I smiled at the beautiful
Bubblegum mermaid's glowing eyes,
As she swam home.

Pranali Patel (8)
Cranford Primary School, Cranford

Fluffy The Delightful, Cute Monster

Fluffy was born in a flat under a mat,
Next to a cat and a fat bat.
She had friends who were as caring as a mother,
But shared like a big brother.
Fluffy and her friends went to the nearest spike,
With their rusty, dusty, and crusty bikes,
They played in a band full of fans,
And smelt like cheese in rotten cans,
Fluffy was good, even though she had food.
She was so fluffy with horns so pretty,
She was a shape-shifting monster,
She could even change into a lobster.
Her eyes were as cute as a puppy,
Not to mention a bunny,
Her skin was as gentle as a mom,
She could never be a bomb.

Reva Theresa Fernandes (9)
Cranford Primary School, Cranford

All About Blobbi

Shadows appear as I sleep,
I wake to see the silhouette that creeps,
It's frightening, it's scary,
That cruel monster that's hairy.
It comes out of the shadow,
I scream then weep.
"Oh dear," comes a sound in the moonlight,
From the monster who is round.
As wobbly as jelly, with a soft belly,
The monster gazes at me and frowns.
"Don't be scared, I'm not at all frightening,
Not as scary as thunder and lightning.
My name is Blobbi,
Looking after children at night is my hobby."
I smile, "How very enlightening!"

Lakshmi Gaur (9)
Cranford Primary School, Cranford

Lillyana Life

Lucky Lillyana had close friends,
Their names were Filly and Dickle,
Dickle liked eating a salty pickle,
Filly liked smelling wonderful lillies.
As you can see, Lillyana is harmless,
And Lillyana is not careless either,
Lillyana is gentle to her friends.
She's from a land which is unusual,
But that doesn't make her weird,
Even if she has hard horns on her head.
Her life as a yeti is wonderful and cool,
Yeti like Lillyana really like eating swirly spaghetti.
Lucky Lillyana has another friend called Filly,
Fun Filly always walked crookedly.

Dhaksha Sundaneswanan (9)
Cranford Primary School, Cranford

The Cyclops Of Darkness

They say he was born,
On the dark side of a mysterious dimension,
This mystical, mythical, and horrid beast,
It as mean as a gargling gorilla,
It is as poisonous as a bee,
It likes to eat yellow yeti but hates pizza,
It loves chaos and possessing people.
One frosty, chilly and creepy day,
There was an alien celebration,
It saw an alien so it quickly dug up a hole,
And threw the alien in,
After everyone muttered, "Thank you."
Then the monster muttered, "No problem."

Fudail Ahmed Ghouri (8)
Cranford Primary School, Cranford

Purple, Hot Frosty

I was playing with my friends,
When I saw a strange alien-like figure,
Walking towards me.
It was small, it looked strange and silly,
I said hello, he said yellow,
I thought he couldn't speak properly.
He was hot, but made out of ice,
It looked friendly and was nice.
It said, "Me like you." I said, "Me too!"
It had spiky spikes,
Its lips were pink,
I thought I couldn't blink,
He had green antennae,
It matched its green eye

Angat Thabure (9)
Cranford Primary School, Cranford

The Monster Stomp

Here comes a monster from Nightmare Isle,
Scaring all the children with a maddening style,
Stomp! Stomp! Stomp!
Should we act slowly or promptly?
It has stiffy, gooey, bloody fangs,
With an extra nice bang,
Its eyes are creepy and white,
When you stare at them, you'll never see the light.
It's very lonely and has no friends,
Don't be sympathetic, it ate them instead,
So, if you need a place to flee,
Go to Shapeshifting Island and be free.

Padmashree Jayshree (9)
Cranford Primary School, Cranford

Pat, The Mat

I have a mat that takes me places,
No need to tie your laces,
Just step aboard and make a wish,
And there you are,
Before you even give your mum a kiss.
Right now, I'm enjoying DanTDM's show in Chile,
Next, I'll go up north to Cali.
But don't worry about the time,
'Cause I'll be back home for supper, before nine.
All this is possible because of Pat,
Who is my favourite mat,
You can come around if you like,
To have a little chat.

Vishnu Chittari (8)
Cranford Primary School, Cranford

Cosmic

She was born amongst the fallen rain,
When dawn struck,
She rose beside the gleaming sun,
Against a sky as clear as a sapphire,
There lay Cosmic the cloud,
With a voice soft and sweet,
And eyes as bright as the day.
She visits the good children,
And knows who's been naughty or nice,
Just like Santa.
Her natural beauty makes people stop and stare,
No wonder Cosmic the cloud and Mother Nature,
Are the best of friends.

Aiza Butt (9)
Cranford Primary School, Cranford

Snail Muncher!

Hi, I am from Stink Bom,
Opposite Zink Com,
All I eat is snails,
That's why I have big, long nails.
I am as stinky as blue cheese,
My favourite food is mice,
It's the tastiest food!
I would also eat round, smelly, sluggy nails.
My name is Stink Snail Muncher,
My friend is Link Leopard Luncher.
You'd better stay with your family,
My eyes glow as bright as a star,
I hate my friend's bar.

Isha Fernandes (9)
Cranford Primary School, Cranford

The Monsters

Stomp, stomp, stomp,
Chomp, chomp, chomp,
We are the monsters,
Who stomp and chomp.
Fiddle, fiddle, fiddle,
Wiggle, wiggle, wiggle,
We are the monsters,
Who wiggle and fiddle.
Smash, smash, smash,
Crash, crash, crash,
We are the monsters,
Who crash and smash.
Write, write, write,
Fight, fight, fight,
We are the monsters,
Who write and fight.

Hemakesh Datta Bavuluru (8)

Cranford Primary School, Cranford

Claw-Blob

C ome from the Earth's core,
L ikes scaring people,
A lways snatches everything,
W as put in the deep blue sea,

B ullies people and hates them,
L ies a lot, especially to the police,
O nly gobbles good people,
B uilds chaos and trouble.

Abdullah Khurram Bhatti (9)
Cranford Primary School, Cranford

Red Dragon

There lived a red dragon,
Whose name was Clang,
He had sharp, pointed fangs.
His horns were white,
He flew all night,
His wings were as hot as the sun.
He was strong enough,
To defeat his enemies with lots of fun,
Although he had a short body,
He was never scared of anybody.

Kalen Fernandes (8)
Cranford Primary School, Cranford

The Adventure Of Pete The Monster

There was a monster called Pete,
And he really loved to eat,
He was a vegetarian,
And didn't act like a barbarian.
He had many friends and absolutely no foes,
And if you counted his friends,
I assure you, there'd be loads and loads.
Pete was also cunning,
And a very clever shape-shifter,
He could change into different forms,
Even to get through a river.
He could fly, he could swim,
He could even make noise,
Whatever he changed into,
Was going to be a decoy.
So if you ever see an animal,
With very strange eyes,
Don't think that's what it is,
It's Pete the monster in disguise!

Harrison Belle-Etoile (9)
Freezywater St George's School, Enfield

The Lonely Monster

There once was a monster,
Who had no friends,
He lived by the seaside,
Where all the land ends.
In the rock pool he lived in,
The fish loved to play,
But when he came out,
They all swam away.
"Please," said the monster,
"I don't mean to scare."
So he climbed out of the rock pool,
And into the air.
When the people saw him,
They all started to screech,
They grabbed their flip-flops,
And ran off the beach.
"Please," said the monster,
"Don't run away,
All I want to do,
Is have fun and play."

He headed to the beach hut,
And knocked on the door,
The people looked out,
And didn't like what they saw.
"Please," said the monster,
"I just want to meet you,
I am really friendly,
I promise I won't eat you."
He went into town,
And walked down the streets,
Until he found a shop,
Full of chocolate and sweets.
"Please," said the monster,
"I have money to spend,
I just want to use it,
To buy me a friend."
"Well," said the owner,
"I have no friends to sell,
But you can buy chocolate,
And that might help."
He went to the park,
And saw all of the toys,

So he walked up,
To the girls and boys.
"Please," said the monster,
"Would you like a snack?
I just want a friend,
I don't want to attack."
So the children ate the chocolate,
And made a new friend,
The monster was happy,
And that is the end.

Tess Fleming (9)
Freezywater St George's School, Enfield

My Kooky Monster

My monster's name is Fern,
She loves to twirl and turn,
She always loves to learn,
About the historic region, Bearn.
Fern likes to eat,
All her favourite treats,
Except from those
Cheeses and greens.
Fern has retro hair,
But she doesn't care,
Even though people stare,
She will still have retro hair.
My monster's name is Fern,
She loves to twirl and turn,
She always loves to learn,
About the historic region, Bearn.

Jenelle Dayo (9)
Freezywater St George's School, Enfield

Roy Roy Is Friendly

Roy Roy is friendly,
His family is very deadly,
Because he is a good monster,
He doesn't know how to slaughter.
This monster may have spikes,
But he can make them go away and has twenty bikes,
He wishes to be on a tropical island,
The only one he knows is Troyland.
He comes from the land of Gitobia,
His sister is called Namibia,
Although Roy Roy is a male,
He is very frail.
The little monster is extremely cute,
He has no friends, so he is quite mute,
Longs to be friends with humans,
Also known as Youhmans.
He's the kindest monster in his land,
He wishes he was grand,
he's different from his family,
Because they smell really badly.

Roy Roy is polite,
I promise he won't bite,
He gets terribly sad,
He has a brutal dad.
Although he can camouflage,
This guy can only scare Raj,
He has one googly eye,
And tries to act sly.

Sheniece Mills (9)
Freezywater St George's School, Enfield

Menacing Monster

Menacing Monster mean but nice,
Her favourite meal was pizza,
But now she likes rice.
She may be sad,
She may be happy,
But don't worry, she's kind of happy.
She sleeps all day,
She sleeps all night,
She's not like owls, 'cause owls don't bite.
She's very fluffy, she's very cute,
Her name is Menacing Monster,
But she can play the flute.

Enaiya Gbadebo (8)
Freezywater St George's School, Enfield

My Monster

My monster is called Ellie,
She lives inside a welly,
She has a big belly,
She is really smelly.
She is really good,
She loves her neighbourhood,
She is brave,
When she is sad,
She hides in a cave.
Ellie is a really nice friend,
She will be with you until the end,
She helps everyone in need,
She always does a good deed.

Elsa Kusi Boateng (9)

Freezywater St George's School, Enfield

The Bogey Man

Bogey Man, Bogey Man,
What a fright.
Bogey Man, Bogey Man,
Crawls in the night.
She might be rising at your school,
Maybe while you're working too.
Her feet never touch the ground,
Her mouth only makes one sound.
Bogey Man, Bogey Man,
What a sight,
I hope she goes away some time.

Helin Kadr (7)
Freezywater St George's School, Enfield

My Monster

My monster's small
But my monster's bad
His eyes are orange
And his skin is red
And he smells so smoky
My monster sleeps in the day
My monster hunts at night
He runs, he jumps
He eats little people
Who don't sleep at night
So here's a warning,
Get to bed!

David Akinseye (8)
Freezywater St George's School, Enfield

Popadopulus' Adventure

As I was walking down the beach,
I saw a monster out of my reach,
I constantly looked up,
And casually said, "Sup?"
The monster told me its name,
So I asked it, "Want to play a game?"
The mosnter agreed with a nod of its head,
I played Marco Polo without a dread,
I saw the monster's fur as blue
As the colour of the sea,
And its eyes as green as the leaves of a tree.
When we'd finished playing,
The monster took me to the sky,
I tried not to cry,
As I was afraid of such a height.
I attemped to hold on tight,
I saw its magnificent wings,
As shiny as diamond rings.
It flew down,
In an old town,
We ate fish and chips,

With lots of different dips.
We flew to my home,
I said farewell and asked him,
To come again before he flew to Rome.
As quiet as a mouse,
I entered my house,
In there, I lay in my bed,
Cuddling my teddy, which was red.

Dishita Tayal (10)
Guru Nanak Sikh Primary School, Hayes

Bhoot Nath A Monster Hunt

(Inspired by 'We're Going On A Bear Hunt' by Michael Rosen)

We're going on a Bhoot Nath hunt,
We're going to catch a tall one,
We're not scared,
But what if he's in the closet?
Better close it,
Slam, slam, slam.
What if he's in the hallway?
Better tiptoe down it,
Tiptoe, tiptoe.
What if he's behind the blinds?
Better open them,
Swish, swish, swish.
What if he's under the desk?
Better go over it,
Swoosh, swoosh, swoosh.
What if he's in the computer library?
Better stomp through it,
Stomp, stomp, stomp.

Argh! It's a Bhoot Nath
What's that you said?
You're tall, but you're fluffy and friendly,
And you want to go to school?
Now we're not afraid of monsters,
So stomp through the computer library,
Walk thorugh the hallway,
Open the closet,
Close the blinds,
Jump over the desk,
And let's get learning mental maths.

Jaskirath Singh Kohli (8)
Guru Nanak Sikh Primary School, Hayes

The Curious

The Curious was born in the river.
He had a fantastic, fluffy sort of skin.
With an eye that's crystal clear
and shiny like the North Star.
He also has a pair of arms and knobbly knees.
With a mouth that stretches
so wide that it goes to the moon and back.
On 15.5.18, he started whistling,
an extremely enticing, eerie tune,
which made all the pictures go *boom!*
and they go back decades.
People also say that they see him
in the back of photos
just waiting to be found
and if you ever look at him
he starts whistling the tune
and captures you in a trance
to lead you out of your home,
never to be seen again.
They also say, if you ever hear his whistle,
something creepy is about to unfold around you.

No one has ever seen The Curious
or knows where he will strike next.
Maybe he'll come to your house,
into your room, waiting for you,
to wake up and scream.

Amreet Gill (11)
Guru Nanak Sikh Primary School, Hayes

Britainly Goes To Britain

"Britainly, you are going to Britain,"
Ordered the king of friendship,
Britainly was shocked,
With her long hands locked,
She obeyed the king,
And set off to Britain magically.
At 8pm she reached Britain,
And gobbled some traditional fish and chips,
She danced graciously,
Moving her gargantuan hips.
All the gloomy people of Britain,
Suddenly danced jubilantly with Britainly,
The magnificent music,
Enriched the whole night, certainly!
While everyone was having a great time,
Never to forget,
She thought that this
Was an auspicious moment,
That no one would regret.
Britainly wobbled and fell,
On the sensational ground,

Everyone made no sound.
However, the people of Britain were grateful,
That Britainly had spread love,
Peace and fabulous friendship,
Rest in peace, affectionate Britainly.

Umber Kaur Kloay (10)
Guru Nanak Sikh Primary School, Hayes

The Beast Who Could Be Your Best Friend

Through the damp, misty forests,
And through the hardest weathers,
A mysterious, giant-like figure appeared,
Climbing into a home in a small village,
And into a warbdrobe.
Tom, a small boy, sat in the corner of the room,
Holding his knees, rocking back and forth,
Feeling alone, he was alone.

A monster possessed him,
Manifested within his body,
Waiting, waiting, waiting,
As silently as a mouse,
Hearing terrifying roars,
Sweating. Not knowing what would happen,
He shut his eyes.

As he opened his eyes, the monster was there,
He was about to scream.
The monster seemed a foul, frightening and a
fearsome beast,

However, he was the most friendliest beast,
They played
And played.

As they were playing, Tom fell asleep,
And the beast never came back.

Amman Virdee (11)
Guru Nanak Sikh Primary School, Hayes

Cuddly, Cute Cuzzy

Monsters, monsters,
They're under your bed,
Monsters, monsters,
They are ruby-red,
Monsters, monsters,
They want to sit on your head.
Monsters, monsters,
They like to smell flowers,
Monsters, monsters,
They don't have magical powers,
Monsters, monsters,
They like to take showers.
Monsters, monsters,
They don't like to fight,
Monsters, monsters,
They have very good sight,
Monsters, monsters,
They're not always right.
Monsters, monsters,
They are all different shapes,

Monsters, monsters,
Some like emerald-green capes,
Monsters, monsters,
Some act like apes.
Monsters, monsters,
They are so fuzzy,
Monsters, monsters,
Their favourite name is Cuzzy,
Monsters, monsters,
They don't like Mr Guzzy.

Amrita Kaur (10)
Guru Nanak Sikh Primary School, Hayes

The Friend Or Foe

This Friend or Foe,
Is very, very slow,
He looks like a Minotaur,
Or a Cyclops,
He has five eyes,
And lots of legs.
This Friend or Foe,
Has a really large toe,
He is pretty fluffy,
And really scary.
He is a clever giant,
Who is very stinky,
He has a big mouth,
Meaning he has a long tongue.
This Friend or Foe,
Came to our village,
He ate up the city,
All in a pity,
He left with all our food,
And let us starve to death.
This Friend or Foe,

Came back to the village,
Gave his support,
And helped to build the city,
He even gave us more food than before,
And led us to our death.
He brought a dragon,
Who destroyed the city,
He destroyed the dragon,
And had a feast.

Paramvir Singh Sekhon (11)
Guru Nanak Sikh Primary School, Hayes

The Gloomy Monster

I thought I heard the monster,
Climbing in the trees,
He had big horns,
Which were partly torn,
I thought I heard the monster.

I thought I saw the monster,
Creeping in the woods,
He had lots of legs,
Stuck in pegs,
I thought I saw the monster.

I thought I touched the monster,
Underneath my bed,
He was very hairy,
But spoke like a fairy,
I thought I touched the monster.

I thought I smelt the monster,
When I flushed the toilet,
It was like old socks,
Stuck on chickenpox,
I thought I smelt the monster.

I know I spoke to the monster,
Standing in front of me,
His big, wide grin,
Fresh from the tin,
I know I met my new friend.
I know I saw the monster.

Sehaj Singh Heer (8)
Guru Nanak Sikh Primary School, Hayes

Miss Pinky's Magical Adventure!

Miss Pinky was born in a magical cloud,
She is a unicorn, but is loud.
She smells like perfume,
And usually wears brands,
And always comes up with naughty plans.
Pinky was sick of being a unicorn,
And wanted to be reborn,
She didn't want to end her life,
So she didn't pick up the knife,
Instead, she rubbed a pearl,
And was gone in a whirl.
She came back as a mermaid,
And there was a big parade!
She loved her new braid,
But then the evil unicorns began a raid.
Mermaid Miss Pinky wanted this to stop,
And then she was home with a pop.
Her eyes slowly opened,

And she was glad it was a dream,
And was glad she was still a unicorn,
So she had some ice cream.

Tia Kaur Mann (10)
Guru Nanak Sikh Primary School, Hayes

High In The Night

With googly eyes like laser beams,
He stood before me, high in the night.
With a dragon-like tail,
He stood before me, high in the night.
With fangs like glass,
He stood before me, high in the night.
He stood before me, high in the night.
With shadows around him,
He crept through the night, high in the night.
With daddy-long-legs like pegs,
He crept through the night, high in the night.
With horns locked with horns,
He crept through the night, high in the night.
With gentle, fluffy fur he cuddled me tight,
All through the night with a bow tie,
He stood with me when I slept,
All through the night.
With a soft sparkly twinkle,
He stayed with me, all through the night.

Maskeen Kaur Heer (10)
Guru Nanak Sikh Primary School, Hayes

Bedtime Monster

When you are sleeping,
And the floor is creaking,
And the door goes bang,
And the window goes whoosh,
The scary, hairy monster says,
"Hi, I'm scary, I'm hairy,
I don't want to cause any fright,
I only come at night,
Because I can't stand the light,
I'll take you on a journey,
Far or near,
As long as you're with me,
You have no fear."

Tarandeep Kaur Jheeta (10)
Guru Nanak Sikh Primary School, Hayes

Basha, Masha And Me

Once upon a time, when I was young,
I saw a pair of monsters,
"La la la," they soothingly sang.
Each day, I used to see them,
At the end of the street,
Dancing with all of us kids, singing to a beat.
Basha and Masha is what they were named,
But their actions showed,
That they were just tamed,
Tranquil and peaceful, is how they always were,
Playing with us boys, always calling us 'sir'.
I do miss them both when I go down my street,
Remembering those good times,
Even during my sleep.
This is the story of Basha, Masha and me,
I hope you get to meet them,
One time, two times, or even three.

Maahn Malhi (10)
Guru Nanak Sikh Primary School, Hayes

Hairy Harry

No one likes Harry because of all his hair,
Whoever he passes gives him a stare,
Except for Emily, who never frowns,
She pictures Harry wearing a crown.
Oh sweet, soft Emily,
Whose nickname is Miss Friendly.
For her kindess, she is known across all the land,
Not like most other kids boring and bland.
Now, back to Harry the star of the show,
A fact that you did not know.
His orange hair that shines so bright,
Glows even more in the night,
Him and Emily are best mates,
And sometimes go out beyond the gates.
Now, this line will make you gleam,
In the night, they had mint chocolate ice cream!

Sukhmani Gill (9)
Guru Nanak Sikh Primary School, Hayes

Ginormica

Ginormica was born in a volcano,
He was as red as a beautiful butterfly,
It went on an adventure.
I saw it in the woods.
People ran and screamed,
But I stood there as brave as a lion,
In fact, I was the lion.
I put my hand out,
As it majestically leaned forward,
My hand touched its magical head,
It was full of scales.
It started to say, "Will you be my friend?"
I thought for a while and said,
"Yes, but why don't you have any friends?
You are very exalted."
He replied, "Because of how I look."
In the end, we became the best of friends.

Ekkam Kaur Saini (9)
Guru Nanak Sikh Primary School, Hayes

Wiggly Woggle

Wiggly Woggle wiggled his wobbly body,
And there he came from outer space.
He stared with his working eyes,
His favourite food is French fries,
His tongue is as yellow as a banana,
His breath is as revolting as rotten eggs.
Wiggly Woggle loves adventures,
And is as curious as a cat,
It has colourful, spotty skin,
And eyes that glow in the dark.
"Hello, can I be your friend?"
He tried and tried,
Going on adventure after adventure,
He never gave up.
"Can I be your friend?"
"Of course you can."
Wiggly Woggle can finally get a friend at the end.

Ria Sunil (11)
Guru Nanak Sikh Primary School, Hayes

My New Friend

Fuzzy was a friendly monster,
That was born in a cave.
It had light blue eyes,
Like the sky that shone in the sun,
Its skin was like a pink butterfly,
Fluttering in the sky,
Its teeth were black like the night,
It was friendly and delightful.
One fabulous day, it met me in the gardens,
And I screamed, "Argh!"
"Sorry," it said, "I didn't mean it."
"It's okay," I said.
As I saw Fuzzy,
He was really a cuddly,
And fluffy, friendly monster.
While the sun set, we walked together,
We were new best friends forever.

Harveen Dhariwal (9)
Guru Nanak Sikh Primary School, Hayes

Slugmaina

My monster lives in Slugmania,
This little fella is very nice,
His flesh is as cold as ice.
I met my monster in a derelict house,
And he was called Furby.
Furby has curly hair,
And his skin is very fair,
And is as strong as a bear.
He went out to the shop,
And someone said, "Stop!"
So Furby walked off to the beach,
When someone asked,
"Do you want a peach?"
Someone gave him one to eat,
Furby found it bitter sweet.
He took his glasses off,
And made people cough.
He then went home
and slept the night off.

Gurjeevan Kaur Dhanjal (10)
Guru Nanak Sikh Primary School, Hayes

Blue The Princess Of Monsters

There was a beautiful monster called Blue,
She certainly didn't belong in the zoo,
But one day, her tummy filled up with goo,
And had to be pulled out with a shovel and glue.

Whatever the matter,
Her teeth would chatter,
As she danced like the Mad Hatter,
Her feet would go pitter patter.

She had beautiful coloured spots,
Which looked like garden pots,
Her friend sold dodgy cots,
With huge, yellow dots.

She had a wide range of brooms,
But all of them lived in her lovely room,
Thankfully, she never met her doom.

Rhiya Verma (10)
Guru Nanak Sikh Primary School, Hayes

The Loving Monster

T om and Ben are his friends,
H e loves his friends a lot,
E ven if they are not with him.

L oves his town, Hayes,
O nly if his friends are there,
V ans he loves,
I n his hometown, there's a park,
N ever is bad,
G ives to the needy.

M y monster loves Glasgow,
O nly if his friends come too,
N ever would he leave his friends,
S aves the needy,
T alks to the needy,
E veryone he helps,
R espects everyone.

Mahaan Singh Virdee (10)
Guru Nanak Sikh Primary School, Hayes

Dodo's Lost

Dodo, jumped out of Nono with an enormous smile,
He searched for a mile,
Until he could hear, "Moo! Moo!"
So he stomped his feet to the tune,
Suddenly, a goat appeared in front of him,
He couldn't understand a thing he said.
The goat sang delightfully,
And Dodo danced lovely.
His feet thundered against the ground,
It shook the Earth beneath and it opened.
Dodo burst into tears of joy,
He embraced the goat like a toy.
He safely went back to his mama,
He promised never to go far away,
In search of Nana.

Simran Singh (8)
Guru Nanak Sikh Primary School, Hayes

The Street Monster Beware

There is a furry-wurry monster,
It lives in a tree,
And when you go past it,
It goes for a wee.
It's near my house,
Outside, on my street,
But if you're nice,
You're in for a treat.
With claws on her paws,
Teeth just like jaws,
Eyes as big as golf balls,
A tail that gives balance.
Ears that can hear an ant fart,
Horns as magical as a unicorn,
That can make the monster disappear.
You can get closer,
Or should I say near?
The monster has a name,
It is Monster, isn't that strange?

Aarian Kaur Purewal (8)
Guru Nanak Sikh Primary School, Hayes

Space Monster!

Like a comet from outer space,
Planning to destroy the human race,
He eats living creatures for lunch,
His army packs a mighty punch.

He is really fat and good for nothing,
His tummy's filled with cotton stuffing,
Drinking rum and being proud of his work,
Little does he know, he's a big jerk.

Because of him, the world's in shock,
He'll be sent back with a very big knock,
You come to Earth, seeking success.
Now you're leaving in a very big mess,

Why do you have so much stress?

Pawandeep Singh Takawal (11)
Guru Nanak Sikh Primary School, Hayes

The Finder

One delightful day on Jupiter,
There was a little guy,
He was very shy.
He got very bored,
So he prayed to the Lord,
That he could build a spaceship.

Four months later...

He built a spaceship,
It was huge like a giant.
He went in the spaceship,
He searched and searched,
Until he found Earth!

He got excited,
He would be famous on Jupiter.
He went back to his spacesip,
Then went to people and said,
"I have found Earth!"
Everybody became friends with him.

Harsweet Randhawa (10)
Guru Nanak Sikh Primary School, Hayes

Illusion

Illusion, Illusion,
Where are you?
A monster with a lag screw,
Born in time,
Favourite hobbies include crime,
Has started to be horrid and rude.

Illusion, Illusion,
What have you done now?
Messed up another party somehow,
He jinxes and curses everyone there,
This behaviour has to stop, it's not fair.

Phew! It is alright,
No more messing around until tomorrow night,
He rests his head on a weeping willow,
Nobody to scare, nothing to do,
Now it is time to doze off, not another boo!

Esha K Khosa (10)
Guru Nanak Sikh Primary School, Hayes

Mohmina's Gang

Mohmina was born on Planet Cribat,
Where they eat a lot of bats,
She is just like a cuddly cat,
She looks like a furry hat.
She is funny and very cheeky,
But in front of her parents, she's very geeky,
Mohmina has a lot of friends,
And they like to hang out at Peaks End.
A few bad monsters came to town,
And made Mohmina and gang act like clowns,
Mohmina went mad and threw a rock.
Unfortunately, it was molten and hot,
The monsters squealed and ran away,
Leaving the gang shouting, "Hooray!"

Ravneet Kaur Khaira (9)
Guru Nanak Sikh Primary School, Hayes

The Planet

He is so scary like Bloody Mary,
He is hairy, not like a fairy.
He is invisible like a small blueberry.
He hates dairy and he has five eyes,
Like five blueberries.
His name is Clawbone, not Gary.
He is not a fairy.
Watch out for people who are scary.
Against Clawbone, you'll be sorry.
When it comes to being scary,
If you're hairy, Clawbone's more hairy.
Clawbone's cousin's name is Parry,
And he is a fairy. Bloody Mary turned scary,
Because Clawbone turned you into a fairy.

Jasraj Singh Bajaj (7)
Guru Nanak Sikh Primary School, Hayes

The Three-Eyed Monster - Harry

One day, in my garden,
Was a three-eyed monster.
He looked scary.
He said, "I am a foster."
He was hairy like a cat,
And was super spotty,
And had sharp claws,
And horns and a tail.
He tried acting nicely,
But when I ran away,
He started to wail.
Then I found out he was friendly,
And we became best friends.
He told me his name was Harry,
We made sure our friendship will never end,
And when people see him,
They will run away,
Because they find him scary.

Sharanpreet Kaur Sahota (9)
Guru Nanak Sikh Primary School, Hayes

The Monster In My Car

There's a monster in my car,
Who sits next to me,
But seems so far.
His bright fire-orange fur,
Makes my eyes blur,
His sapphire-blue eyes,
Make him look scary,
But truly, deep down,
He's a fairy.
His crooked teeth,
Have never touched beef,
Because, in the morning,
He's always in a rush,
His smelly mouth,
Has never stopped talking,
And is very loud.
He has never had any friends,
Because of how he looks,
And he always has a disappointed face.

Sehajveer Sethi (11)
Guru Nanak Sikh Primary School, Hayes

The Devilish Monster

Kiara was born on an exotic island,
She had baby pink, fluffy fur,
And illuminating, crimson eyes.
Kiara had electric blue spots,
She left the gorgeous island,
Kiara was the rudest monster ever.
She met me in the jungle,
I tied Kiara to a tree.
Her razor-sharp fangs cut it open,
Before she escaped,
I pushed her onto the floor.
"Finally!" the people cried.
"The monster's gone!" they all shouted,
"You are our hero!"
"Thank you all."

Nimret Kaur Jandu (11)
Guru Nanak Sikh Primary School, Hayes

The Frightening Monsters

Night fell as I woke up,
Argh! There are monsters in the wall!
There are monsters in the closet,
There are monsters in the hall,
There are monsters underneath my bed!
There are monsters behind my door!
They could be green, red or blue,
The monsters all shout, "Boo!"
My bed is an island,
With monsters everywhere!
Until the sun comes out,
Then they all disappear,
I saw monsters but did they see me?
Don't tell anyone, they'll be scared, you see!

Simleen Kaur Sachdev (11)
Guru Nanak Sikh Primary School, Hayes

The Scary Friendly Monster

He's a monster who loves to eat lobster,
He's eaten many creatures,
But his favourite one is lobster,
And he's the only one who,
Can turn his frown upside down.
His favourite colour's brown,
He's found many towns,
And wears a lot of gowns.
His heart pounds,
As if he's had a heart attack.
He has a bendy back,
He has a lack of money,
And a pony called Tony.
He is very lonely, and is also bony,
He has a house with a big, fat mouse.

Harvir Singh (9)
Guru Nanak Sikh Primary School, Hayes

The Sneaky Animal

Once there was a monster,
Who had sharp claws like a lobster,
He was mad,
Just like his dad,
He had poisonous antennae.
He could also breathe fire,
He robbed banks and stole shiny things,
Nobody could stop him,
Except the frightening things!
One of them had ghostly skin,
Which meant his brother had razor-sharp claws,
That means the cat had paws.
This combination was too much for the monster,
So he gave in to the police,
He was then put behind bars.

Jagdeep Singh (9)
Guru Nanak Sikh Primary School, Hayes

The Mysterious Green

I wake up and open my blind,
I look outside to see...
Wait, what do I find?
A bright green figure,
Who doesn't look very kind,
In a sparkling tutu,
Eating a lime?
I think twice, then open the door,
He looks around and then to the floor,
He wonders and then asks,
"What's this place?"
He looks perplexed,
Oh my days!
He's covered in slime, I wonder why.
Oh, look again, there's also grime!

Gunveen Kaur Arora (11)
Guru Nanak Sikh Primary School, Hayes

Jeffy The Cloud!

Jeffy Jeff once fell out of a cloud,
Everybody was scared and ran a mile,
But Jeffy was not vile,
He was very nice,
And only ate rice.
He slept early every day,
Apart from in May.
He melted on the bay,
And slipped into the water,
"Argh!" he raged,
Becoming a monster.
He ate everything he could,
But he was sucked into the air again.
"Bye Jeffy, see you again in May! Not!"
Said the children.

Gurpreet Singh Rajwansi (10)
Guru Nanak Sikh Primary School, Hayes

A Shadow In The Street

A normal night on Bakers Street,
Late shoppers running out and in
Of the cute little shops, tidy and neat,
But, a strange sound overpowered the din.
A distant scream that seemed to meet
The eeriness of the feeling,
That crawled up your skin.
A menacing, black shadow that seemed to eat
The happiness and light, even the darkest sin.
It was the shadow.
The shadow of no more,
The scream of the end,
The shadow of the dead.

Attar Kaur Hanspal (11)
Guru Nanak Sikh Primary School, Hayes

Atlantia On The Track Of Evilness!

This evil creature,
Born in the sea on a thundery day,
Harassed each and every animal or creature.
She was know by the oceans,
As the evil mermaid,
Even a shark could escape from her.
She had claws like shark's teeth,
Deadly horns like vampire teeth,
She captured her prey,
Tortured it, and ate it on the third day.
Who is she? What is her name?
It's Atlantia Cobalt.
Never meet her, or make friends with her.

Navneet Kaur (11)
Guru Nanak Sikh Primary School, Hayes

My Monster My Friend

My monster has five eyes,
My monster can fly high,
He can fly in the sky,
He flies faster than a jet.
My monster is very clever,
And he can be very smart,
He can also be very sneaky,
But he can shoot laser beams.
And sometimes he can get very mad,
So I have to tell him off for being bad.
He lives in a volcano,
On his own, sometimes he sits.
Although he can be very naughty,
He is my monster, he is my friend.

Karanbeer Bhullar (8)
Guru Nanak Sikh Primary School, Hayes

The Merfluff Adventure

The Merfluff was born in the ocean,
It has sea-foam green skin,
And shiny blue eyes,
That twinkle in the night sky.
It smells like salty sea water,
And has pearl-white teeth.

The Merfluff was on an adventure,
Across the clear blue sea,
But then she hurt her fin.
Oh, what a tragedy,
She swam to the surface,
And then she met me.
I helped her,
And we became merfriends,
Across the sea.

Arshpreet Sehdev (9)
Guru Nanak Sikh Primary School, Hayes

Monster Friend

M arvellous,
O h so sweet,
N ever rude,
S teps up from cute cats' furballs,
T reats everyone like a friend,
E ven loves you and me,
R eally, please don't run away.

F orever free,
R eally loves sprinting,
I love this monster,
E ven loves to fly,
N ever scary,
D ay to night, she will always be my fab friend.

Kirtan Kaur Dhaliwal (10)
Guru Nanak Sikh Primary School, Hayes

Monster, Monster

Monster, monster, hiding in the dark,
Stay there and don't come out,
If you come out, don't shout,
Where are your manners?

Monster, monster, hiding in the dark,
Play nicely with us,
Being nice isn't a fuss,
We can be as friendly as can be.

Monster, monster, hiding in the dark,
If you come out, be nice,
We can play games with dice,
Come out, come out, don't be shy.

Harjan Singh (11)
Guru Nanak Sikh Primary School, Hayes

The Evil's Transformation

There was once a lonely man,
Who had no big fan.
All he had was a watch,
Which was stolen by a man.
That very moment,
That very second,
Turned him into The Evil.
He stole many items,
Necklaces, books and watches,
Which made him a monster.
He made a rocket ship,
He went to Monster Land,
The Evil stole many things there.
As everyone knew he was a robber,
He became The Devil!

Manchit Singh Grover (11)
Guru Nanak Sikh Primary School, Hayes

The Troon

The Troon was found,
And born on the moon,
And didn't know how,
To use a spoon.
He didn't go outside,
He wanted to go to Mars,
Or go outside,
And see all the stars,
As, inside,
He could only see jars.
His family didn't own any cars.
he wanted to own a van,
But inside, he only saw,
A frying pan.
He also wanted a cat,
That would always sit on his mat.

Jaiveer Chana (9)
Guru Nanak Sikh Primary School, Hayes

The Monster Mystery

It crawled and crept out of a little corner,
Its eyeballs were as big as the moon,
I tried not to look, but they were round and big.
Today I will not fear it.
It came slowly slithering towards me,
I tried looking but it was too dark,
I could only see its dark black eyes,
And its white, sharp teeth.
Bam!
Light shone upon him, and there it was,
The dreadful snake monster!

Simar Kaur (10)
Guru Nanak Sikh Primary School, Hayes

I Am Hairy Harry

I am Hairy Harry,
I am from Saturn,
I am hairy like a poodle,
So I can keep warm like a polar bear.

I am Hairy Harry,
My friend is Maggie Mary,
My other friend is Loopy Larry,
We love to have new friends,
And play hide-and-seek.

I am Hairy Harry,
I would go to a hotter country,
So I could be a bit warmer,
And find new friends,
I am Hairy Harry.

Simrit Somal (10)
Guru Nanak Sikh Primary School, Hayes

Five Eyes And Me

Five Eyes, Five Eyes,
A friendly creature,
Who inspires me like a teacher,
Cheerful, no matter what,
His smile puts my tummy in a knot.
He's furry and cuddly,
And jumps on me suddenly,
He's never without a smile,
On his fuzzy, sweet face,
Sometimes I feel like,
He's from outer space.
5 eyes looking at me,
All different colours,
Filled with glee.

Navkiran Kaur Virdee (10)
Guru Nanak Sikh Primary School, Hayes

The Fellow

My name is Mellow,
They call me fellow,
And I am yellow,
I say hello.
They say I'm a dragon,
That loves a wagon,
I live in a gigantic house,
With a big mouse.

I'm very short,
So I need support,
They say I need to talk,
But instead, I walk.
I go potty,
When I turn spotty,
I love the pool,
Because it's so cool.

Jasmeet Kaur Sekhon (9)
Guru Nanak Sikh Primary School, Hayes

The Monster Who Went To School!

A monster once went to school,
He ate all the books,
And put his things on other people's hooks.
Everyone was petrified,
Whilst teachers were terrified.

He ate all the cake,
And replaced it with a fake,
He ate all the moose,
And replaced it with juice.
This was the monster,
Who once went to school,
And made everyone a fool.

Harkamal Singh (9)
Guru Nanak Sikh Primary School, Hayes

Marvellous Monster

My lovely monster is cute and chubby,
Who is as red as a ruby,
His skin is so fluffy and very hairy.
He loves to play around and make merry,
But he weighs a ton, his name is Mattoon.
Thank god, his farts are now quiet and few
Oh, my Lord this is news
He is a monster, he is a Mobster
But hates eating lobster
I love my monster, I love my monster.

Falguni Sodhi (10)
Guru Nanak Sikh Primary School, Hayes

Messy Boppy!

M essy Boppy does it again,
E very day making a mess,
S ometimes here,
S ometimes there,
Y et he doesn't pick it up.

B oppy doesn't bother,
O nly sometimes is he funny,
P lop! He drops his books in the pond,
P icked up by a good girl,
Y et, he is still is not organised!

Harsimran Kaur (10)
Guru Nanak Sikh Primary School, Hayes

Not Cool

The monster's name is Zommer,
He's not cool, he's a fool,
He has seven eyes,
And loves chips that are fried.
He's as long as a giant,
And as nasty as a Briant,
He's green and likes to lean.
He comes from Imalasa,
And he has a brother and sister,
As he is the older,
He comes to notice,
That he's a monster.

Gurleen Singh (10)
Guru Nanak Sikh Primary School, Hayes

Mctroy

Mctroy came from Hell,
To cast a spell,
He is a boy,
Who's filled with joy.
Fearsome fangs,
On his hands,
Stinky, smelly breath,
With lots of theft.
Wolfish brains,
With lots of pain,
Looking scary,
As he's so hairy.
Spikes on his tail,
Like ants in a trail,
Oh dear, oh dear,
I'm full of fear!

Mannat Kaur Kohli (9)
Guru Nanak Sikh Primary School, Hayes

My Best Friend

The monster was born in a hot place,
It had bright colours,
It smelt like flowers,
It was nice and helpful.
It left the island and went to his friends,
It was kind and made people happy,
But it met me on the beach.
I helped my friend,
His skin went bright like the sun.
"Hello," it said.
We played together and laughed.

Sukhman Kaur Sandhu (10)
Guru Nanak Sikh Primary School, Hayes

When I Met Petunia!

Petunia, my new friend,
Petunia, my new friend,
When I met her in the Indian Ocean,
She was with her awesome friends
Petunia is cheeky, chubby, clever and naughty,
We are very good friends,
And on the first day,
We swam together for three hours,
One week after Petunia and I went home,
I was still as tired as a cavewoman.

Chavleen Chopra (8)
Guru Nanak Sikh Primary School, Hayes

Fanger And The Floating Boat

There he was, sitting under a tree,
He was very hungry, so he ate a bee.
One day, a monster called Fanger saw a ball,
He was very clumsy, so he knew he would fall.
Fanger was soon getting tired,
So he lay by an oak,
There he saw a boat!
He jumped in the boat and watched it float,
And off into the distance he went.

Khushpreet Hoonjan (10)
Guru Nanak Sikh Primary School, Hayes

Appearance Is Not Everything

M agnificent and pretty like a unicorn.
A lthough, she is very stinky, like an unwashed, rotten piece of corn.
L ovely she may look, but inside, she is evil.
I dentifying it is even easier than trying to escape prison.
E xtending out her wings, she flies away. Soon she will be seen during night and day.

Simran Kaur Phull (11)
Guru Nanak Sikh Primary School, Hayes

The Hairy Monster

There once was a hairy monster,
And it was spotty with antennae,
It lived in a volcano,
Under the lava,
And had no friends.
To everyone, he was a monster,
Everybody thought he was as hairy as a bush,
But then the monster proved to them,
That it was a friendly monster.
Then, they all became friends.

Sanam Sachdev (9)
Guru Nanak Sikh Primary School, Hayes

Naughty Trew

Trew the monster was from the volcano park,
He has six eyes and lots of legs,
And is really naughty.
It has lots of monster friends like humans,
And one time, it blew fire on a Sikh school.
I would run away if I saw Trew anywhere.
I saw Trew in a park once
And when I hit him, he turned green.

Rythamdeep Thind (7)
Guru Nanak Sikh Primary School, Hayes

This Halloween

This Halloween,
I may be seen,
When you're getting a fright,
It gives me might,
This Halloween.

This Halloween,
You'll see me,
In blue and green,
With candy.
My face is a snake,
But my body is furry,
And orange eyes will gleam,
This Halloween.

Dipneet Kaur (11)
Guru Nanak Sikh Primary School, Hayes

The Crazy Monster

I once saw a monster,
Who was eating a lovely toaster,
His lovely name was Vinck.
He didn't even dare to think.
Sadly, one day, he decided to be lazy,
So then he sent the whole house crazy!
After he called his family and friends,
And told them to meet his new pal, Firenze!

Avneet Kaur Chawla (7)
Guru Nanak Sikh Primary School, Hayes

My Monster

My monster has shiny blue eyes,
And can fly through the sky,
He has a red face,
He can breathe fire,
He isn't a liar.
I saw him on the street,
Sitting on a seat,
My monster is my friend,
And our friendship will never end,
Because he's my monster.

Ramneek Kaur Grewal (10)
Guru Nanak Sikh Primary School, Hayes

The Dradle

The Dradle was a friendly creature,
And it would never have to eat,
It flew around on tiny wings,
Doing its own things.
But some people did not like this beast,
And decided to have it for a feast,
But the Dradle did not approve of this,
And decided to fly away.

Jagdeep Singh Virdee (10)
Guru Nanak Sikh Primary School, Hayes

Vampirealina

The beast on the train,
Sometimes stood in the pouring rain,
Waiting for someone to notice her.
Because of her fur,
No one knows that she is a vampire.

Her fangs are as white as snow,
Sometimes she wears a bow,
Nobody knows
She is a monster.

Angelina Kapur (8)
Guru Nanak Sikh Primary School, Hayes

106

Threa The Questionable

Threa, Threa,
Why so clumsy?
Threa, Threa,
Who lost her arms?
Threa, Threa,
Who has three-eyed friends just like herself.
Threa, Threa,
Where are you?
Threa, Threa,
Why so stinky?
Threa, Threa,
Threa.

Jasveen Kaur Singh (9)
Guru Nanak Sikh Primary School, Hayes

Laser Lazy

L aser beams,
A ggressive,
S melly,
E ager beaver,
R apid rager.

L azy legs,
A ngry as a bull,
Z eus' power,
Y awns a lot.

Amraj Singh Dhaliwal (10)
Guru Nanak Sikh Primary School, Hayes

The Shy And Excited Monster

My monster is fluffy,
And can do a little puff.
But once he got lost,
And I was heartbroken,
Looking for him in the woods.
Finally, my cute, cuddly monster,
Had arrived back in town!

Nitika Sharma (8)
Guru Nanak Sikh Primary School, Hayes

Leviathan Wrath

His name was Leviathan,
He wanted to control the world,
He travelled to Earth,
Right after his birth,
Will he control Earth?
Yes, he will,
But first, he will kill.

Mannat Sedana (8)
Guru Nanak Sikh Primary School, Hayes

Dobby

D isgusting and dirty,
O nly one way to avoid it is,
B ananas.
B ananas. He hates the smell of bananas.
Y uck. The only thing he eats is muck.

Seerat Monjal (9)
Guru Nanak Sikh Primary School, Hayes

My Fuzzy-Looking Monster

Oh monster, oh monster,
I am looking at you,
Fuzzy and green,
Oh what do you do?
Fuzzy-looking monster,
Am I scaring you?
Cute at first,
Ugly at last.

Tegh Kaur Rao (9)
Guru Nanak Sikh Primary School, Hayes

Toxic Viper

Shoots venom like a sniper,
It's very hyper,
Smells like a diaper,
Wails like a bagpiper,
Colourful like a candy striper.

Looks like a snake,
Gets a tummy ache,
Cries like a mandrake,
Eats steak-flavoured cake,
Makes people quake.

Born in nuclear waste,
Always snot-faced,
Good manners misplaced,
Fangs are debased,
Never uses toothpaste.

Harrison Sykes (8)
St Michael's CE Primary School, Brigadier Hill

Changeover

Boy monster has a bright green hat,
shiny chestnut eyes, gold shoes,
and a pair of tiny glasses.
He loves flying in his
blue spaceship. His
favourite thing is
to get sticky.
He is the
stickiest
thing
ever.
Boom! The next day, he is a lady!
Girl
monster
has a red
sparkly dress,
bright blue eyes,
black ginormous eyelashes,
and lovely pink lipstick. If she didn't,
she would look so much like a monster.
You would be able to find out.

Emeline Gee (8)
St Richard Reynolds Catholic College, Twickenham

She'll Come Back In June

She sparkles like the stars,
She glistens like the moon,
She comes from Mars,
But I know she will come back in June.
She is fluffy like the clouds,
And she gets rid of my doubts,
She is a little pink blob,
Who stops my sobs.
She is as smart as me,
She is my key to be free,
She shimmers like the sea,
After all, she is my creation.
She stomps on the green grass,
And she giggles,
She hums like a hummingbird,
As we look around for fun.
But when she goes back,
I look for her tracks,
And I see the sparkling stars,
Along with the glistening moon.

Lakeisha-Jayne Seenauth (8)
St Richard Reynolds Catholic College, Twickenham

Cute Gury, My Monster Friend

Cute Gury is furry and kind,
Cute Gury came from his galaxy,
My furry friend is adorable,
With many eyes and mouths,
He has two friends over all the time,
And one of them is me!
I love having a monster friend,
It's always scary but fun!
He takes me to his galaxy,
To play with his friends,
Cute Gury is a monster,
But this monster is kind and furry,
Furry and kind!
I love his mind,
I love his fun games,
He is the best monster I know,
Funny and furry,
Furry and kind,
This is my friend, Cute Gury!

Anne-Marie Kostov (8)
St Richard Reynolds Catholic College, Twickenham

Freaky Four Arms

Freaky Four Arms is a child eater,
He eats children.
He lives underground in the stinky sewers.
Freaky Four Arms is a smelly,
Slimy, squishy, slug-like monster.
When his giant, wobbly tummy starts to rumble,
Watch out children!
His googly eyes will catch you by surprise,
Even though you don't know he is there,
He is glaring from his lair,
Licking his lips and flopping along,
On his tentacle legs as he moves
Towards his prey.
His four arms are ready to catch
Any children in the way.
His gigantic mouth swallows them whole.
With a bubbly burp, he rubs his tummy.
Before daylight comes, Freaky Four Arms
Quickly flops back to the sewers,
And he waits for his next victim.
Warning all children, don't go near the sewers!

Milo Ketteringham (7)
St Richard Reynolds Catholic College, Twickenham

The Visit To Jupiter

My name is Simon, I'm seventeen years old,
I have twenty-one fun, furry friends.
I have five eyes as bright as a shooting star,
I am half monster, half ghost, and horribly hairy.
Tomorrow is my birthday, I am eighteen,
I am going to visit Jupiter,
I am as excited as a puppy with a bone.

My birthday is finally here!
I am now flying to Jupiter,
Two long hours have passed, what a journey,
My six arms are as tired as a dog after a walk.
I have arrived! What an amazing place.
Everything is as green as a grasshopper.

What was that I just heard? We are not alone.
I turn around and see little bossy Bob,
And the rest of my furry, fab friends!
We have a super surprise birthday party for me,
There is a cake as detailed as a picture,
Monster biscuits, slimy slugs, my favourite,

And mushroom pizza! It is the best party ever!
But now it is time to go home, boo hoo.

Maisie Marsden (9)
St Richard Reynolds Catholic College, Twickenham

Vampia's Holiday

Vampia is furry and as black as coal,
You won't want to be out late,
She'll suck up your soul!

She hypnotises witches,
And throws them in ditches,
She comes from the Dark Lands,
Where ducks have fangs.

She has scar-patterned wings,
Oh, aren't they beautiful, my darklings?

But she came to Earth for a holiday,
She said, "Nice to meet you,"
But people just said, "Go away!"

Except one little girl said, "Are you okay?"
"No," a sobbing voice said,

"I really wanted to make them giggle.
I never really sucked up souls,
But now I'm just in a pickle."

All of a sudden, the people
Came out of their homes,
And said, "Nice to meet you,
You're not a meatball with foam!"

Elsie Kinch (8)
St Richard Reynolds Catholic College, Twickenham

My Grrrr

Every night, when you go to bed,
You may have dreadful dreams in your head,
There, in Brainstorm Kingdom, I live,
But you don't have to believe.
I'm furiously friendly King Anger,
Who loves to thunder with anger!
I fume, I groan, but I like jokes:
"What did the angry monster
Do when he got his gas bill?
He exploded!"
Sometimes, I'm a bit lazy,
But I love being crazy.
My best friend is Charming Chatty Cleverhorns,
Who stays as cool as a cucumber,
And teaches me how to control my anger.
"Don't be sulky, don't be moody,
Do some yoga, drink a tasty tea with soda,
Dance and smile, run for a mile."
So after a while, King Anger changed,
Into a crunchy, munchy panda!

Olivia Swiderska (8)
St Richard Reynolds Catholic College, Twickenham

Munchy The Monster

This is a poem about Munchy,
Munchy likes to munch, munch, munch.
Munchy loves treats,
His favourite food is meat,
And sometimes sweets.
He lives in Alaska, in a deep, dark cave,
Even though he's scared of the dark,
He is very brave.
One night, there was a storm,
With lots of snow,
Munchy was trapped in his cave,
With nowhere to go!
Munchy was hungry, so he had to dig a tunnel,
He was in a bad mood, he really wanted food.
He dug for a while, and had a nap,
When he got up, he wanted a snack.
Munchy was happy when he got out,
He had brunch and lunch.
Munchy was happy when he could munch,
Are you happy when you can munch?

Finbar Harris (8)
St Richard Reynolds Catholic College, Twickenham

Monster Friends

This is a monster,
Who lives on planet Bongster,
He has no friends at all,
So plays alone with a ball.
He's good, but always
Gets the worst pud.
When monsters go near him, they go,
"There's the stinky bin!"
When he does art,
The monsters throw tarts.
I met him once and said,
"Do you want to go
On an adventure with me?"
"Okay!" he replied, and on the way,
He fell into a bubbly lake,
And all the flies disappeared,
"I am scared of water!" he said.
I pulled him out,
And went back to school,
He made lots of friends.

"Thank you, you're magical!"
He said as I walked home...

Bianka Krystina Szabat (9)
St Richard Reynolds Catholic College, Twickenham

The Flubaball's Monster Vacation

On the beach, underground, furry and round,
Lives the Flubaball, who I call Fluffy,
And his furry family.
They were going on vacation,
But there was a complication,
Everyone was running,
When they were oh so very friendly,
All they had was some food,
And their pet, Bendly.
The manager threw them a key,
And claimed to need a wee,
At least twenty-one people hurt their knees,
So off the Flubaballs went to Hotel P.
They were kicked out as they came into view,
So they went to a bog and hopped like a frog,
Went to the forest and had fun with Uncle Norris,
And had a delicious picnic and went home,
And checked the underground garden gnome.

Bosley Brown (8)
St Richard Reynolds Catholic College, Twickenham

Sadeye The Lonely

Sadeye was lonely and had one friend,
And he didn't live very far from the bend,
In school, he didn't talk or write or do that much,
His only friend was, oh yes, lunch!
He really wasn't that clever,
And he was no one's piece of treasure,
His feet were so large so he didn't have any shoes.
At break, he would sit on the bench,
And get the blues,
Nobody ever knew why he was sad,
Somehow, he didn't get mad.
His body was red,
And he was not allowed to eat bread,
His horns and feet were blue,
Sadeye's feet were like ducks, but times two,
And he had long, oval eyes.
His bed was red, so he was in disguise.

Saskia Fahey (9)
St Richard Reynolds Catholic College, Twickenham

My Friend Jelly

J elly is my friend,
E ven when he's mean,
L oves to play football,
L oves to play cricket,
Y esterday, he was kind.

M ean sometimes,
O n Saturday, he threw a chair,
N ot a good choice,
S o people were rude,
T o my friend Jelly,
E xcept when he said, "Sorry."
R unning followed by crowds of people.

F ollowed him to Jelly World,
R acing wobbly cars,
I n Jelly's land,
E veryone gave him a big hug,
N obody was mean again,
D isco and jelly party for everyone!

Lewis Fitzgerald-Monk (9)
St Richard Reynolds Catholic College, Twickenham

Good Dreams

There is a monster in my cupboard,
She came to say hello,
She wanted to take me somewhere,
But I didn't want to go.
One day, I woke up,
And next to me,
I saw something strange,
I looked a bit closer,
And saw it was a hairy monster.
I tried to run away,
But the fluffy monster
Held my arm and said,
"Don't be scared of me,
My name is Sally,
I'm a very nice and clever monster."
Sally had fluffy, orange hair,
A big mouth, with a few teeth,
One eye big, one eye small,
And two short hands.
The next night, I had a dream,
Where me and Sally became good friends.

Nikola Nycz (8)
St Richard Reynolds Catholic College, Twickenham

Last Night

It had been a very busy day,
And, as I crawled into bed,
And lay down my head,
I began to dream.
I met a monster whilst eating lobster,
He was slimy and green,
But not at all mean.
He had a freaky eyeball,
In the centre of his head,
And sat chatting all night,
At the end of my bed.
He told me his name was Oliango,
And his favourite food was mango,
So I got him some mango,
And he said, "Fandango!"
But of course, I didn't know what it meant.
As the sun rose, the monster with no nose,
Had to go back to his planet called Nauglios.

Charlotte Rose Ball (8)
St Richard Reynolds Catholic College, Twickenham

The Brown Giant

As tall as a mountain,
As smelly as a sweaty sock,
The giant looked down,
From the magnificent rock.
The grass giant's ferocious fangs,
Stuck out from his mouth.
The smelly, stinky giant,
Flew through the sky,
Spreading its wings,
And jumping through the air.
He flew to Monsteryork,
And made lots of friends.
One day, he said, "Roar!"
Which, in our language,
Means, "Good morning my friends,
Please come over for tea!"
After tea, he went up to bed,
And had a nice dream,
Of his nice, cuddly ted.

Harry Ibbs (8)
St Richard Reynolds Catholic College, Twickenham

Fantastic Bodge

Bodge is my monster's name,
He is small, round and very tame.
My monster has green fur on his head,
His pillow is covered when he gets out of bed.
He has two blue eyes that serve him well,
His all-seeing eye, the future does tell.
Bodge has a little, round, pink tummy,
Wild berries and nuts he finds very yummy.
He was born in a forest near my house,
He lives in a tree and is as quiet as a mouse.
During the day he plays with a bear,
He loves playing truth or dare.
At night he sleeps in a tree,
It's a long way down if he needs a wee.

Sienna Minhas (7)

St Richard Reynolds Catholic College, Twickenham

Madam Fashion

There was a monster called Madam Fashion,
All she liked was fashion.
She lived in a village far away,
Its name was Funny Fashion.
Everyone wanted to play,
But Madam Fashion was too shy today,
It was like she was ignoring them.
She came home sad, and saw her dad,
Drinking tea with sugar.
She went to him and said, "What should I do?"
Her father said to make a bow.
She went to her fashion room,
And got out lots of fabric and started sewing.
"Done!" she shouted in excitement,
There was her sparkling bow.

Liza Coimbra (8)
St Richard Reynolds Catholic College, Twickenham

My Friend The Monster

I met a monster one day, when I went to the park,
I was amazed to see, he was tall and ugly,
And it had five eyes. It was purple in colour,
With yellow spots.
When I approached him, he was very funny,
And had a big hole in his tummy,
He picked me up and called me Mick.
I laughed at him and he laughed at me,
I said to him, "My name is Charlie."
He put me down and started to roll and roll
All over the grass with laughter.
He got up and said to me, "Let's go Harley,
And find Mrs Farley."

Charlie McKenzie (9)
St Richard Reynolds Catholic College, Twickenham

The Invisible Monster

M r Invisible lives on Monster Island,
R etelling stories from long ago.

I nvisibility is so clever to him,
N ever gets angry at anyone,
V isiting his friends nearly every day.
I n Monster Land, he loves playing hide-and-seek,
S ometimes, he gets lonely.
I n Monster Land, he thinks it's the best place,
B ecause of all his friends, he's so happy.
L etting all his friends play fun games,
E veryone is happy with their monster friend.

Rosetta Piercy (9)
St Richard Reynolds Catholic College, Twickenham

ters

Have you ever seen a monster?
They are big and scary and rather hairy.

Have you ever seen a monster?
They have scratchy claws,
And ear-splitting loud roars.

Have you ever seen a monster?
They have pointy teeth that tear at meat.

Have you ever seen a monster?
They have fiery breath that's a recipe for death.

And if you want to see a monster?
If you want to see a monster,
If that is what you plea,

For if you want to see a monster,
Just come around for tea!

Huxley Kinch (9)
St Richard Reynolds Catholic College, Twickenham

The Monster Who Came To Breakfast

Early one morning, there was a knock on the door,
Nobody knew what it was for.
We opened the door and a monster walked in,
From eating our trash and our bin,
He now wanted more to fill his tummy,
He was very pleased to see something yummy:
A cinnamon swirl, a croissant and orange juice.
I can't believe this monster is loose.
He gobbled it up in just one bite,
This monster really is a fright,
I can't believe how much he can eat.
He then walked out and laughed,
As he skipped down the street.

Theo Corth (8)
St Richard Reynolds Catholic College, Twickenham

Tickells' Time

T ickells is a friendly and fluffy monster,
I know he's from a clam planet, as he's always said it.
C ome on, what shall we play?
K ick the ball? Catch the ball? Climb?
E verything, he can do.
L et's have a fun time,
L et's do some fun things!
S omething we have to do.

T ime to draw!
I 'm going to draw Tickells!
M aybe even a robot with Tickells in it!
E rm, I'm going to draw where he lives.

Nerea Whitmore (9)
St Richard Reynolds Catholic College, Twickenham

Shorty Sporty Steve

Friendly Steve has silky skills,
He's the sportiest monster you'll ever meet,
He may be short but he'll prove you wrong,
He shoots and scores all day long,
The other monsters can't stop him,
The goalies can't save his shots,
He scores every match,
There is a secret in his spots,
They make him super at sport,
His sister Sarah is the same,
He'll always challenge you to a game,
Shorty, sporty, spotty Steve,
Loves scoring all day long.

Daniel James Atkinson (8)
St Richard Reynolds Catholic College, Twickenham

Bert The Hairy, Scary Monster

I always knew there was something
Hiding under my bed,
I think he comes from Mars,
He has no friends,
And he is as evil as a daring devil,
I have named him Bert.
He is hairy, scary,
And as ugly as a giant tarantula.
He has three eyes and no legs,
But he has three enormous fangs,
He has big, bushy eyebrows,
And fur the colour of fire.
Sometimes I hear him snoring,
As loudly as booming thunder,
Oh how I wish he would go back to Mars!

Freya Hughes (9)
St Richard Reynolds Catholic College, Twickenham

The Batall

The Batall was born on a cloud,
When it was tall, it fell from the clouds,
And landed in a volcano.
Then it started growing spikes.
Batall got red-hot skin and left the volcano,
Because it went on an adventure,
To make people sad, and it insulted everyone.
Until it went to the park.
It fell and landed in a hole that I dug.
Then, everyone at the park said,
"You saved us!" I smiled,
With my clean teeth and sparkly, brown eyes.

Miguel Ángel Mendoza Estrada (7)
St Richard Reynolds Catholic College, Twickenham

The Monster With Five Eyes

The monster with five eyes can fly,
The monster with five eyes is very tall,
The monster with five eyes is stinky,
The monster with five eyes has razor-sharp horns,
The monster with five eyes has horns with laser beams,
The monster with five eyes is good,
The monster with five eyes' name is Jake.

Casper Hillier (8)
St Richard Reynolds Catholic College, Twickenham

Monster Toast

My monster's name is Toast,
She loves to eat a Sunday roast.
She is always very cheeky,
People think she is very freaky.
Toast is purple and furry,
And her ears are long and curly.
She lives in a cave by the lake,
During the day she bakes a cake.
During the night her purple eyes twinkle,
Onto her plants, water she sprinkles.
She loves to play with her BFF Chuck,
They play catch with a rubber duck.

Liana Minhas (7)
St Richard Reynolds Catholic College, Twickenham

Meet Flaming Skull

Meet Flaming Skull,
He's really mean,
Don't say hello,
He won't be keen.

As big as a lorry,
Tough as a rock,
He hates everything,
From trees to a croc!

Racing through cities,
Climbing on shops,
One thing you'll see,
Are his bruises and knocks.

After you've read this,
This poem right here,
Be very cautious,
Flaming Skull might be near...

Finlay Kinch (9)
St Richard Reynolds Catholic College, Twickenham

Monsters Under My Bed

When it's time for slumber,
I start to hear thunder,
Then my silky, soft friend,
Comes out to defend.
I start to hear Shimmer's soft, soothing voice,
Suddenly, I'm not scared any more.
Then my tummy begins to rumble,
Shimmer runs into the kitchen.
Shimmer appears back, holding a bag of crisps,
I eat them slyly, so Mum doesn't notice.
I'm not scared any more, Shimmer is here.

Scarlett Nicol (9)
St Richard Reynolds Catholic College, Twickenham

Blob

Blob is blue and blubbery,
Slimy and slobbery,
He comes from Mars,
And likes chocolate bars.
Blob is lonely,
He is an endangered species,
The rest are gone,
They all crumbled to pieces.
Blob had no friends,
Except for me,
He visited Earth,
And came round for tea.
He is slow though,
We don't go far,
Just to the shops,
To buy more chocolate bars.

James Hazard (8)
St Richard Reynolds Catholic College, Twickenham

My Friend Squishy

My friend Squishy has three special friends:
Nutkin the squirrel, Daisy the blossom,
And me. My name is Ben.
Squishy loves to help Nutkin, Daisy and me,
To get ready for winter, you see.
He helps us to gather our food,
Nuts, seeds, and berries to store,
In a secret hole,
Where no one can find them.
The hole in the tree was so high,
That no one could even spy it.

Euan Fitgerald-Monk (7)
St Richard Reynolds Catholic College, Twickenham

The Tiny Terror!

The Tiny Terror is small and scary,
When he's around, you must be wary,
Because he's as fast as a rocket.
Keep your eyes at the floor,
Because you don't want him
Jumping up any more.
Beware of the poisonous spike,
If you don't, you could get a fright.
Now you've heard about this tiny mite,
You might not get a bite.

Liam Jack Jeffers (9)
St Richard Reynolds Catholic College, Twickenham

Gob's Victim

M enacing claws ripping into your flesh,
O ut of this world exists his home planet,
N othing can stop him from paralysing you,
S uspicion lurks around the monster's myth,
T errorising the city,
E xtinguishing people's lives as they sleep,
R acing heart beats will be terminated.

Benjamin Norman (8)
St Richard Reynolds Catholic College, Twickenham

Pickles

Pickles Pickles loves lots of tickles.
He lives in a cupboard and eats all the pickles.
But you think he's cute and fluffy and pink,
When it is dark and no one is awake,
He hides under your bed and sets up a trap.
And when you wake up in the morning,
You will hear a *boom! Splat!*

Maria Shakaj (8)
St Richard Reynolds Catholic College, Twickenham

Monty The Monster

One day, when I was feeling sad and blue,
Monty the monster appeared out of nowhere.
He danced around and jumped up and down,
His crazy, blue hair flew all over.
He took me to the zoo, to look at the animals,
Our favourite was the magnificent monkey,
Swinging branch to branch while eating a banana.

Ethan Nicol (7)
St Richard Reynolds Catholic College, Twickenham

Sad Rock

The Rock Man grew and grew,
He smashed up the sofa,
And smashed up the loo,
As the children cried, "Boo hoo!"
I asked it to be my friend,
Then, it stopped.
And it got smaller and smaller,
And put back the sofa,
And put back the loo,
And it said, "Sorry."

Jack Bunney (8)
St Richard Reynolds Catholic College, Twickenham

Not So Scary

Scary was from Planet Linky,
His best friend was Binky,
The problem was Scary wasn't scary,
Instead, he was rather hairy.
One day, Binky and Scary,
Set off on a journey,
To find Planet Shun,
But read it wrong,
And ended up on the sun!

Isabel Bunney (8)
St Richard Reynolds Catholic College, Twickenham

Monsters

I have a friend called Yeti,
He's big, purple and furry,
And when he gets happy,
His cheeks go soft and puffy.
When it's raining outside,
We splash in all the puddles,
Then go inside for hot chocolates,
And lots of lovely cuddles.

Ella Payne-Traverso (8)
St Richard Reynolds Catholic College, Twickenham

Gruff

Gruff lives in the sea,
He's slimy and blue,
And has a horn like a thorn.
He's angry and bad,
And his eye glows red,
When he's terribly mad.
The fish in the sea,
Are not very happy,
As Gruff is always so snappy.

Albert Connors (7)
St Richard Reynolds Catholic College, Twickenham

The Green Monster

He's big and green,
And terrible and mean,
He appears at night,
When all is quiet.
With only one eye,
And with his wings, he's a bird,
A great, big, fluffy bird.
His name is Bedue.

Luca Gasparini (8)
St Richard Reynolds Catholic College, Twickenham

Hairy Monster

Monsters are hairy,
Monsters are scary,
This monster is blue,
He is wearing shoes.
He has a cat,
And he sat in a boat,
And he was not there for long,
And now he is gone.

Len Mundow (9)
St Richard Reynolds Catholic College, Twickenham

The Singing Monster

I am so tiny,
I come from the sky,
But I cannot fly,
And I don't have wings,
But I love to sing!

Susanna Benedetto (7)
St Richard Reynolds Catholic College, Twickenham

The Shadow

Something is hiding at night,
It will give you a fright,
It hides in your room,
And *boom!* You are gone.
It's scary, when everyone is gone,
He will throw a bomb,
It says, "Red fish, blue fish, two fish."
Now he is dead. The sea is red now,
There are no fish, now there's no you.
When you hit your head on the door,
The light turns off, now you're on the floor.
Its name is Shadow, he is not a crow,
He is a dragon that has been forgotten,
If you say 'Shadow', he will come for you.
Goodnight, it will be your last.

Mohamed Hussein (9)
Viking Primary School, Northolt

The Tech Ghost

Lurking in the shadows of the day,
The Tech Ghost goes into your house,
But it doesn't go inside to play,
It doesn't want to find a mouse.

It wants to steal all of your tech,
So it can make a terrific tech tool,
So it can go on a fun trek,
A journey as long as a swimming pool.

A while after it'll come back,
And it won't forget to take your tech,
If you hide it, it'll get it back,
So don't hide it in a small shipwreck!

Jaasiel Opeoluwa Olosinmo (9)
Viking Primary School, Northolt

The Black Angel

Some monsters are red,
Some monsters are blue,
Beware, he will kill you in bed,
Watch out, he might bite you!
Beware, he might suck your blood,
If you're lucky, he will spare your life,
He'll chop off your head with a thud,
He'll kill you quickly with all of his might.
He's so rich with diamonds and gold,
As he rules his cauldron empire.
Because he is so cruel and bold,
Be careful, he will kill you with a deafening choir.

Raheem Kaoud (9)
Viking Primary School, Northolt

The Omega

Some monsters are red,
Some monsters are blue,
You'd better hide under your bed,
Because they're coming for you!
Its robotic eyes can see from a long distance,
Its dragon-like claws drip with juicy, red blood,
It's useless to try and put up a resistance,
If you lie I'll make a thud.
If it knows that lied,
Then there really is nowhere to hide,
For very soon, you will surely be dead,
Will this fearsome freak be satisfied?

Yakub Mustapha (9)
Viking Primary School, Northolt

The Evil Eye Demon

Lurking in your deepest, darkest fears,
A horrible creature is coming for you,
He could be anywhere, even behind you!

He is big and round and it has sharp teeth,
And likes to eat.
The dragon likes to stomp around with big feet.

The dragon is as big as a giant,
It breathes fire with burning hot flames.

The dragon is horrible and hideous,
It is big and bad, that is why
People call him the Evil Eye Demon.

Emuovweoghene Clement Ewruie (9)
Viking Primary School, Northolt

Scratchy The Stinky

Scratchy the Stinker shoots
Very stinky bombs,
She likes to eat a lot of cobs,
She is pretty stinky,
She likes the colour pink.
Her eyes are as red as blood,
She can cause a big flood,
She has purple dripping down,
She even met a clown.
She can walk as fast as a car,
She can eat a chocolate bar,
She is so nice,
Like some cute mice.
She can make your day,
With her cute smile,
She can run a mile.

Wiktoria Orzycka (9)
Viking Primary School, Northolt

Little Monster's Reactions

Little Monster is as ungrateful as you,
Don't make him shout because he'll moo!
Sometimes the bullies call him 'Spider',
And when he gets mad, he'll go higher.
Don't be rude to him because he'll chew,
On you and guess what, afterwards,
You're going to smell of poo.
Don't mess with him because he'll beat you,
After he beats you, you'll smell like goo!

Mustafa Osmani (8)
Viking Primary School, Northolt

The Evil Naughty Giant

The naughty, hairy giant is so scary,
An unknown creature
From an unknown maker,
It lies waiting beneath,
The loathsome beast is called,
The Naughty, Hairy Giant.
Its horrifying eyes watch from long distances,
It had two sticky horns popping out of his head,
Like eggs popping out of his forehead.

Yonis Arab (8)
Viking Primary School, Northolt

YOUNG WRITERS INFORMATION

We hope you have enjoyed reading this book – and that you will continue to in the coming years.

If you're a young writer who enjoys reading and creative writing, or the parent of an enthusiastic poet or story writer, do visit our website **www.youngwriters.co.uk**. Here you will find free competitions, workshops and games, as well as recommended reads, a poetry glossary and our blog.

If you would like to order further copies of this book, or any of our other titles, then please give us a call or visit **www.youngwriters.co.uk**.

Young Writers
Remus House
Coltsfoot Drive
Peterborough
PE2 9BF
(01733) 890066
info@youngwriters.co.uk